# Townspeople and Ranchers

## of the California Mission Frontier

Jack S. Williams
Thomas L. Davis

The Rosen Publishing Group's
PowerKids Press™
New York

*To our parents and families who have always
supported our interest in the missions,
and especially to our wives and children*

Published in 2004 by The Rosen Publishing Group, Inc.
29 East 21st Street, New York, NY 10010

Copyright © 2004 by The Rosen Publishing Group, Inc.

First Edition

Editor: Joanne Randolph
Book Design: Corinne Jacob

Photo Credits: Cover, p. 47 drawings by Father Ignacio Tirsch, courtesy of the National Library of the Czech Republic; back cover,
p. 12 courtesy of Jack Williams; p. 4 reproduction of a painting by Cal Peters, courtesy of Tumacacori National Historic Park;
p. 5 reprinted from *José de Gálvez Visitor-General of New Spain (1765–1771)*, University of California Press; pp. 6, 20 courtesy of
the Karpeles Manuscript Library; pp. 8, 17, 32, 50 courtesy of the Bancroft Library, University of California, Berkeley; p.13 Cindy
Reiman; p.16 illustrated by Jack Williams; pp. 21, 22, 23, 38 Photo Collection/Los Angeles Public Library; pp. 25, 37, 48 © George
Ancona; p. 27 Tarlton Law Library, University of Texas School of Law; p. 28 History Collections, Los Angeles County Museum of
Natural History; p. 29 photo © Cristina Taccone; pp. 30, 31 courtesy of La Purisima Mission State Historic Park, California, photos
© Cristina Taccone; p. 34 Museo Naval, Madrid; pp. 39, 40 courtesy of Mission San Antonio, photos © Cristina Taccone;
p. 42 Dover Pictorial Archive Series; p. 44 © Erich Lessing/Art Resource, NY; p. 52 © Richard Cummins/CORBIS; p. 54 © 2002
Geoatlas ® all rights reserved; p. 57 original art reference by Jack Williams, recreation by Corinne Jacob.

Williams, Jack S.
Townspeople and ranchers of the California mission frontier / Jack S. Williams and Thomas L. Davis.
    p. cm. — (People of the California missions)
Summary: Describes the daily life of townspeople and ranchers at early California missions.
Includes bibliographical references and index.
  ISBN 0-8239-6284-9 (library binding)
1. Missions, Spanish—California—History—Juvenile literature. 2. City and town life—California—History—Juvenile
literature. 3. Ranch life—California—History—Juvenile literature. 4. Pioneers—California—Social life and customs—Juvenile
literature. 5. California—Social life and customs—18th century—Juvenile literature. 6. California—Social life and customs—
19th century—Juvenile literature. 7. California—History—To 1846—Juvenile literature. [1. Missions—California—History. 2.
City and town life—California—History. 3. Ranch life—California—History. 4. Frontier and pioneer life—California. 5.
California—History—To 1846.] I. Davis, Thomas L. (Thomas Leslie), 1950- II. Title.
  F864 .W737 2004
  979.4'02—dc21
                                                                                            2001007872

Manufactured in the United States of America

# Contents

# The California Frontier

California has always been an area rich in natural resources. No one would have ever imagined such wealth in 1769, when the first Europeans moved to the region. The story that follows tells how California's first towns and ranches came into existence, and how their inhabitants began to work toward a brighter future.

By 1750, Europeans had established control over much of North America's coastline. Rival kings now turned to the lands that had not yet been claimed. Carlos III, king of Spain, sent José de Gálvez to Mexico, part of the Spanish Empire, to figure out a way to protect his claims to California. Gálvez told the king that he would have to act soon or give up his plans for developing the territory forever. Carlos ordered Gálvez to occupy California immediately.

*José de Gálvez, pictured here in a 1775 portrait, was in Mexico from 1765 to 1771. When he decided to start missions in Alta California, he asked Father Serra to head the first settlement.*

How could Gálvez achieve this objective? Mexico did not have enough people, money, or soldiers to colonize and protect California. Despite the lack of resources, Gálvez believed that Spain could extend its control over California. He developed a daring plan. Gálvez ordered that California be

◄ *The Anza Expedition, which brought dozens of new families to settle California, prepares to leave from Tubac in 1775. Led by Juan Bautista de Anza, the expedition's final destination would be San Francisco.*

*This is the title page of the Grant of Nobility given by King Carlos III to José de Gálvez to reward his service in the Americas. The text inside says, in part, ". . . Having passed personally in 1768 to the California peninsula . . . (Adding) to my domination more than 500 leagues of Alta California . . . established missions up to the port of San Francisco."*

colonized using missions. A small group of Roman Catholic Franciscan priests, headed by Father Junípero Serra, would establish these outposts of the Spanish Empire. The Franciscans were a group of Christians who lived together as a community and usually worked in the fields of religion and education, and helped poor people. In Mexico, they had often acted as missionaries who tried to persuade Indian peoples to become Christians. In California, Father Serra's followers were expected to transform the Indian people into loyal Spanish settlers. In the eyes of the government and the

Franciscans, a person had to be a Roman Catholic to be considered civilized. Therefore, California and its native peoples had to convert to Christianity. When this had been accomplished, the Spanish government hoped that the Indians would become colonists and protect California for Spain. The final part of the plan was that the Indians-turned-colonists would become prosperous and send money to Spain, in the form of taxes.

Gálvez's plan did not call for large numbers of settlers to move to California. Besides the missionaries, he knew that he would have to send some soldiers to protect the priests and keep away rival Europeans. These men would live in military colonies called presidios. The settlements were to be built at various harbors along the coast. These locations would provide the soldiers with excellent positions from which to confront an invading enemy army. The missions had to be built in areas that were close to the military outposts, because unfriendly Native Americans could easily attack the priests and the Christian Indians. In 1769, the Franciscans and the army established the first combined presidio and mission at San Diego. The following year, the newcomers built a similar settlement at Monterey.

Spanish government officials hoped that the presidios would be able to get all the food they needed by growing it or by purchasing it from the missions. However, by the time that San Francisco Presidio was founded in 1776, it was clear that this plan was inadequate. Felipe de Neve, the governor of California, asked permission to establish another kind of settlement in the province. He wanted to build two towns, or pueblos, to support the army.

*A presidio was established at Monterey in 1770. After 1815, it developed into a large open town. In 1826, it received its charter as a regular pueblo. This image of the emerging settlement titled* The Presidio and Pueblo of Monterrey, Upper California *was made by a visiting British sea captain named W. Smyth in 1827. It was first published by R. N. Day and Hoghe, lithographers to the queen.*

In 1777, the first settlement in California that was inhabited exclusively by colonists who were not soldiers was established at San José. Four years later, the town of Los Angeles was created by another group of settlers.

From the start, the missionaries strongly objected to the new settlements. The Franciscans did not trust the colonists from southern California. The missionaries were afraid that the lack of government supervision would allow the towns to become centers of lawlessness. The Franciscans were especially concerned that the townspeople would teach the Indians bad habits, such as gambling and drinking. They believed that the newcomers would eventually try to steal the Indians' lands, and make the native peoples their slaves.

The missionaries wanted to bring the Indians the best of their civilization. Father Serra argued that the towns would bring the worst qualities of the European way of life to California.

The creation of towns also went against Gálvez's original plan to settle the region using presidios and missions. Governor Neve recognized these objections. He created rules to limit the potential problems. Neve ordered that only farmers be allowed to live in the towns. They were given small areas of land that were not being used by the mission Indians. Nobody in the town was permitted to operate any other kind of business. There would be no stores, saloons, or gambling halls. The presidio commanders were placed in charge of the towns. Anyone who hurt Indians or stole anything from them was to be swiftly punished. Neve argued that, for all practical purposes, the two new outposts were simply extensions of the presidio system. The governor felt that as long as these rules were enforced, the towns would not cause any problems for either the army or the missions.

Six years after the first town was established at San José, five retired soldiers asked Governor Pedro Fages for some land on which to raise horses and cattle. In 1784, Fages gave them large land grants in areas that were not being used by the mission Indians or the army. Here, the colonists raised herds of animals that they sold to the government. The settlers called the new outposts *ranchos*, or ranches.

This upset the mission fathers even more. These new ranches had less supervision than the towns! Furthermore, the missionaries demanded to know who had given the governor the right to give away Indian land. Fages responded by telling the Franciscans that the properties would be returned to the native peoples whenever they needed the land. The soldiers from the presidios would prevent the ranchers from breaking any laws. He reminded the priests that the king needed horses and cattle to keep the presidios going.

In the ten years that followed, the two frontier towns remained relatively unimportant parts of the colony. In 1795, San José and Los Angeles included a few hundred farmers who grew crops and raised animals that were sold to the presidios. The number of ranches did not increase. Most of the land of California remained in the hands of the missionaries. The majority of the non-Indians lived in the presidios.

By 1796, it had become clear that San José could not produce enough food to feed the military bases at San Francisco and Monterey. Diego Borica, the governor of California, decided that the time was right to establish another town. The settlement of Branciforte was established on the shores of Monterey Bay, near Mission Santa Cruz. Borica also decided to grant additional ranches to retiring soldiers and townspeople. Between 1795 and 1796, twelve new land grants were made. This number increased slowly. By the end of the Spanish rule in California in 1821, the number of large grants that had been issued topped thirty-six.

The town and ranch population grew very slowly. After 1781, no large groups of people were sent as colonists from Spain or Mexico. Many of the retired soldiers and their families preferred to live at the presidios. Most of the few new people who came to the region had jobs at the military colonies. It was very difficult for a person to get rich by ranching. The government controlled the prices of the animals so that they would always be able to buy the animals and grain needed for the presidios. As long as the government was the only buyer, there was little reason for the ranchers to increase the size of their herds, or for people at the presidios to want to move into the towns. The only way that the ranch and town population could grow was for their families to have more children.

When Mexico became independent from Spain in 1821, California became a territory of the new nation. Mexican officials abandoned the old policies that had been used to govern the region. The rules that prevented people from setting up businesses in the towns were no longer relevant. Dozens of new land grants were issued. For the first time, people could buy and sell anything they wanted at any price. Some of the settlers started making a lot of money. The growing population of townspeople and ranchers were jealous of the mission Indians. Some of their elected leaders worked hard to eliminate the Franciscans, and get their hands on the natives' lands. By 1835, the missions and presidios were gone. A new age of ranches and towns had come to California.

# Learning from Oral History

Information about life in California's first towns and ranches is often difficult to find. To understand the past, historians study the written records and artifacts that have been left behind by early settlers. Cultural anthropologists study living people to learn more about how things were once done. Archaeologists study the traces of earlier human activity, such as broken pieces of pottery and other artifacts.

Historians who specialize in oral history talk to the descendants of the early families to learn more about life in old California. The descendants are people who have family members, such as great-great-great grandparents, who lived in the region when it was a part of the frontier. The people who lived long ago are called ancestors. Of course, no one who lived in the mission days is still alive. However, they have left with their descendants important clues about the past.

Most people learn about their ancestors from family stories. As people grow older, they pass on these stories to their children. Children repeat the stories to other family members. When they die,

*Old pieces of pottery give an archaeologist information about when a community existed and how the people in that community lived.*

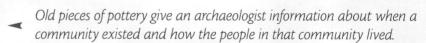

*To learn about the California missions, an oral historian, as represented here, conducts interviews with people whose ancestors lived in one of the mission communities.* ➤

the stories live on through their descendants. These descriptions of what happened are called oral history.

Specialists in oral history have to be careful about using the information that they collect. Some people make up stories. Others change things around, or forget certain important facts, such as the year someone was born. To make sure the information is accurate, the historians have to confirm as many facts as they can through written records, and through the stories that are told by other families.

# Who Were the Townspeople and Ranchers?

Spanish government officials often called the townspeople *pobladores*, or *paisanos*. They referred to the colonists who owned the large livestock estates as rancheros. During the early days of the colony, the people who lived in these settlements, along with those who lived in the presidios, tended to call themselves *Norteños*, or Northerners. After Mexico became independent of Spain in 1821, the same group often described themselves as Californios, or Californians.

The early colonists came from many parts of the Spanish Empire. In 1769, Carlos III's kingdom stretched around the globe. It included large parts of South America, North America, Asia, Africa, and Europe. Very few of the town dwellers or ranchers were born in Spain. Instead, most were the children, grandchildren, and great-grandchildren of Spanish-born colonists.

The people who moved to California married individuals from many different races. These people included Indians, Africans, and Asians. By the time California's towns and ranches were built, nearly two out of every three settlers represented a mixture of these groups. They came from many different races, but the settlers shared a common way of life, language, religion, and goals. They were united in their desire for land and economic opportunity.

Most of the founders of Los Angeles had African blood. Blacks who lived on the California frontier were nearly all born free. Some of the African peoples' ancestors had moved to Spain in the Middle Ages. Other blacks had come to Spanish America as slaves. Spanish laws made it possible for every slave to make money by working on Sundays. Many slave owners gave their human property bonuses in cash for doing extra work. Some of the people eventually saved enough money to purchase their freedom. After they left their masters, the ex-slaves moved to the frontier to start new lives.

Many people had moved to the California frontier from all over Mexico and the southwestern United States. Some of the Indians had come from what had been the Aztec Empire. Many native peoples had come from Sonora and Baja California.

*An Indian of Baja California is returning from a fishing trip and another is on his barklog boat.*

A smaller number of the colonists had come from Asia. Many of these people had been born in the Philippines, islands that were also ruled by the king of Spain. Most of the Asians who had come to California were sailors.

◄ *Pueblo de Los Angeles, the second town to be established in California, was founded in 1781.*

Many of the first pioneers who lived in Los Angeles and San José were retired soldiers from the presidios. However, from the start, Spanish royal officials made some special efforts to recruit townspeople from Mexico.

To get people to live in the towns, the government offered the colonists certain gifts. Every family received a small piece of land for growing crops, a site for a house, tools, and several cattle. Some of the immigrants even received clothing. The townspeople did not have to pay taxes for several years.

Some of the people who lived outside of California liked the government's offer, and so did many of the retired soldiers who lived at the presidios. They liked the idea of making money away from the watchful eyes of their military commanders and priests. The towns became home to some of California's wildest, most adventurous colonists.

# How Were Towns and Ranches Organized and Built?

California's towns and ranches were organized and built differently from the rest of Spanish America. Most Spanish colonial towns were founded by groups of settlers. In California, the government established the towns. Most towns had their own priests and government officials. In California, the army ran the towns, and the missionaries served as priests. In most regions, the town squares served as marketplaces. In California, no one who lived in the towns was allowed to engage in trade. The early ranches were also different from those of the rest of the frontier. Most land grants were purchased from the government and could be owned forever. In California, grants were often given as rewards to retiring soldiers, and the land had to be returned if the mission Indians needed it. Most of the people who owned large land grants in other parts of Spain were very wealthy. In California, most ranchers were poor, hard-working cowboys. Another difference in California was that only army and mission officials were legally permitted to buy or sell grain and cattle.

## Founding a New Town

The first step in building a settlement was to find the right location. The townspeople needed plenty of land for growing crops, grasslands to feed animals such as cattle, and water. An ideal town site was one that was located

En la Ciudad de los Ángeles á treinta de Enero de mil setecientos ochenta y cuatro años.

El Sr. Don Gaspar de Portola Coronel de los R.s Exercitos Governador Político, y Militar en esta Ciudad, y su Jurisdicción por su Mag.d Dixo: Que por el correo Semanario á recivido la Superior resolución antece.te Y en su vista, para q.e tenga el cumplimiento del...

mando se publique por Vando en la forma regular en las partes acostumbradas, y dho. se practicó; en la presente As.ta de Gu.a para su constancia en todo tiempo: así lo proveyó, mando y firmó.

Gaspar de Portola    Ante mí

Lorenzo Anez de Saldaña
S.rio de Gu.a y Justicias

En la Ciudad de los Ángeles en treinta de Enero de mil setecientos ochenta y cuatro se publicó este Vando en la forma y lugares acostumbrados siendo testigos Don Juan Joseph Perez de Merino, Don Christoval Blanco y Pedro Soxo vecinos de esta Ciudad doy fee.

Saldaña

Retardación.    El Navío

Por mandado de S.E.a

Sobre Retardación, y el Navío nombrado de abierto en lug.r del S.or Felipe de 17 de Diz.e de 83

Sobre Retardación, y el Navío...
lug.r del S.or Felipe de...

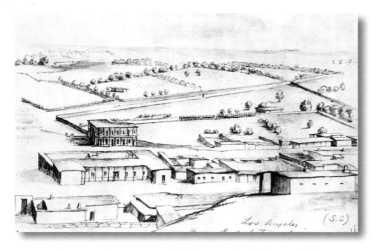

*Los Angeles was nestled in a valley below a hilltop, as shown in this 1847 drawing of the town and vineyards. This is one of the earliest drawings of the Pueblo de Los Angeles.*

on a hill near a river. Once the right area had been selected, army officials divided the property into a variety of smaller units. Some of the grassland was set aside for feeding the community's animals. Every family received land for farming.

The army officials also laid out a town square, or plaza, surrounded by house lots. One side of the square was usually set aside for government use. Here, the colonists would build a police station, a jail, and a residence for the soldiers. The towns also had city halls, in which army officers and town officials would hold meetings and trials. The army officials gave each family a piece of land that was large enough for a home and a yard.

## Founding a New Ranch

Once the governor gave permission for a new ranch to be created, army officers would mark the ranch's boundaries. The person who received the land grant usually selected the place that would serve as his headquarters. The person generally chose an area near a stream or river, with plenty of

*Gaspar de Portolá (1723–1786) was the commander of the expedition to colonize California. He explored many regions, including those where the early pueblos were later built. This letter was written by him 14 years after he left California, when he was serving as the governor of Puebla, an important city in Mexico.*

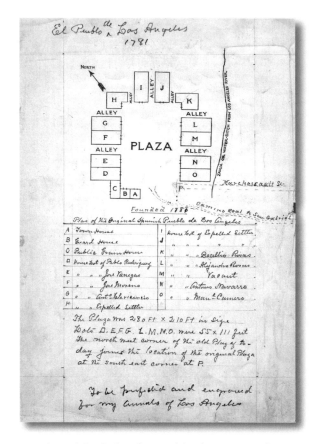

The original plan for Pueblo de Los Angeles included a town hall, guardhouse, public grain house, and lots for its settlers. The plaza area was 280 feet (85 m) by 210 feet (64 m).

grass for their animals to eat and land that could be used for farming.

In contrast with other kinds of settlements, there were no government rules about organizing a ranch's buildings. Most of the owners decided to live with their families in the towns or presidios. They hired workers to take care of their animals, or visited them part-time. The buildings that the ranchers created usually consisted of a few huts, or crude adobe houses, surrounded by fields, and a corral.

## Building the Towns' and the Ranches' Houses

Once the army had laid out the plans for ranches and towns, the colonists were ready to build their homes. Huts, called *chozas*, were set up as temporary shelters. The colonists made the walls of these structures out of a combination of logs, reeds, brush, mud, and leather. They made the roofs from straw or grass, and mud.

The colonists hoped to replace their huts with stronger houses made from earth or stone as soon as they could. To build a permanent home, the settlers had to manufacture thousands of unfired bricks, known as adobes. Mud and straw

*In 1840, an adobe house like this one stood at the entrance to the Santa Monica Canyon. Adobe houses could be found all over the California mission frontier.*

were used to make the bricks. The townspeople constructed the adobe walls on top of foundations made from stones and mud.

A number of factors complicated the progress of the townspeople's construction efforts. At San José there were constant shortages of building materials. As a result, most of the settlers continued to live in huts until 1821. The settlers of Los Angeles and Branciforte also experienced severe shortages of resources. By 1800, some adobe houses had been completed, but few had the new kind of waterproof tile roofs that had been introduced to California in 1780. Instead, the impoverished people of Los Angeles smeared tar that they collected from the beaches onto their dirt roofs to prevent water from pouring in during the rainy season. The tar made the houses smelly. In the summer it ran down the walls and dripped from the roofs. The buildings of the early towns and ranches were never as nice as those of the presidios or missions.

# Government

## The Comisionados

Before 1824, the presidio commanders appointed commissioners, or *comisionados*, to rule the towns. Elsewhere in the Spanish Empire, elected mayors, called *alcaldes*, and town councils, called *ayuntamientos*, governed such settlements. The soldiers who were placed in charge of the outposts were usually sergeants or corporals. Most of the men were married, and they lived with their families in the towns. California's mayors and city councilmen, who were called *regidores*, worked as the army commissioners' aides. Through 1824, the presidio commanders directly supervised all aspects of life in the towns.

In many ways, the army commissioners were like the marshals and sheriffs of the American West. The presidio commanders required them to enforce all of the king's laws. It was not easy to be a town commissioner. According to the missionaries and presidio commanders, the townspeople were more likely to break the law than anyone else in California. Sometimes they drank too much. Some townspeople gambled away everything that they owned. There were many fights that ended in serious violence. Some townspeople even captured Indians and tried to make them into slaves. The army commissioners arrested town settlers who broke the rules. They put the people who were guilty of small crimes into the stocks, or made them spend

*Despite the commissioners' enforcement of laws that were designed to prevent trade, small amounts of goods were traded between settlers at improvised markets, as shown in this reenactment.* ➤

time in jail. Murderers and other serious criminals were sent to the presidios, where the base commanders tried them.

One of the biggest jobs assigned to the army commissioners was the operation of the towns' granaries. At the end of the harvest season, the commissioner would weigh the grain using heavy iron scales. He would pay each of the families for their produce. The towns' fields usually produced a lot more food than was needed by the settlers. The army transferred most of the surplus food to the presidios. No one was allowed to keep any of the harvest. During the year, the settlers bought back whatever food they needed for their own use. The government controlled all the prices.

Not all the town commissioners did a good job. Some of them adopted the bad habits of the people who lived in the towns. A few army commissioners were worse than the criminals that they were supposed to catch. Instead of enforcing the law, they used their positions to take advantage of the other townspeople.

## Elected Officials

The king gave the colonists of San José, Los Angeles, and Branciforte the right to elect their own town councils and mayors. These officials helped the army commissioners to govern the towns. The town councils and mayors had many jobs. They often acted as lawyers and judges when there was a trial that involved a small crime, such as being drunk. If there was a sign of serious danger, the mayor sounded a drum. When the men of the community heard

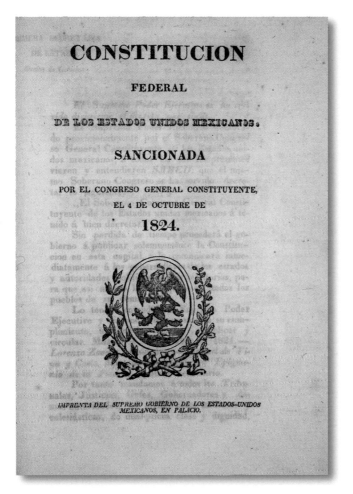

*The Mexican Constitution was adopted in 1824 by the newly independent Republic of Mexico. The new set of laws brought many changes to the frontier regions, including California.*

this call, they rushed to the town square. Unfriendly Indians or wild animals, such as grizzly bears, often attacked the outposts. There was always a danger of fire or flood. Once the community had assembled, the town officials took charge. The mayors carried special batons as a symbol of their authority. It was considered a great honor to serve as a town official.

Before 1824, the mayors and councilmen took most of their orders from the army commissioners. When the Mexican government adopted a new constitution, it eliminated the role assigned to the army in town government. The elected town councils took on direct responsibility for most law enforcement. In almost every way, the towns now ruled themselves.

# Daily Life of a Frontiersman

There was a certain order in the lives of the frontiersmen who made the towns and ranches their homes. The morning began with a hot breakfast served at home. The food included tortillas made from corn or wheat and a kind of porridge made with corn, called *atole*. Some families enjoyed the luxury of hot chocolate.

After breakfast, the men and the older boys went off to tend to their crops and animals. At about noon, they took their lunch break. This was the main meal of the day. In addition to tortillas, the colonists usually enjoyed a thick stew called *pozole*. Other foods that were eaten at lunch included fish, shellfish, and beef. If they were lucky, the family might enjoy baked bread, or a roast chicken.

After lunch the townspeople spent the next few hours at rest or socializing. At about three o'clock, everyone went back to work and continued their efforts through the late afternoon. During the evening, the settlers consumed the final

*Maiolica, a kind of pottery made with tin oxides, was used by the early Spanish colonists. These specimens were made after 1835 and were found during the mission era.*

◄ *Alexander Francis Harmer (1856–1925) painted Doña Maria Coronel grinding corn on a metate for tamales and tortillas.*

meal of the day. It consisted of the same kinds of foods that were eaten at lunch. After the meal, they enjoyed various forms of entertainment before going to sleep at about 12:00 A.M.

## Farm and Ranch Work

The men who lived in the towns were first and foremost farmers. Their main crops were corn, wheat, and barley. Some townspeople also had fields of vegetables and orchards of fruit trees and olives. Because the areas around the towns were so dry, the farmers had to bring water to their crops. They did this with a system of canals, called acequias. The settlers spent a great deal of time building and maintaining these ditches. The townspeople had to work very hard from sunrise to sunset during the planting and harvesting seasons.

Most of the townspeople kept small herds of cattle, horses, mules, goats, and sheep. The ranchers had larger herds of cattle and horses. The men that worked on the ranches spent most of their time with their animals, rather than farming. The settlers' livestock provided milk, cheese, and meat, as well as many other useful items, such as leather, horn, and wool. These materials were used to make clothing, various kinds of containers, blankets, belts, saddles, and dozens of other products.

*Here is a spur from Mission La Purísima. Spurs were attached to a horseman's boot and were used to help control the horse.*

*This is a replica of a saddle tree from Mission La Purísima. A saddle tree was made from a wood skeleton, sometimes reinforced with metal, which was then covered in wet rawhide to make a saddle. When the rawhide dried it was painted or varnished to prevent rot and insect damage.*

The ranches and towns did not have barns in which to shelter the animals that grazed in the open on nearby grasslands. The cowboys, who were called *vaqueros*, had to look out for their livestock nearly all the time, so they spent most of their days on horseback. There were many dangers, including wild bulls, grizzly bears, and other ferocious animals. There was always the possibility that the herd might stampede at sudden sounds, such as thunder. Unfriendly Indians often stole horses and cattle. Being a cowboy was dangerous, hard work.

Life in the ranches and towns did not always go smoothly. Occasionally, the parts of California where the immigrants lived had whole years when little or no rain fell. These dry periods brought many hardships. The crops would die unless they received water. The settlers often dug new canals in a desperate attempt to ensure that there would be enough food for their families. Because there was not enough grass for the livestock to eat, the colonists would have to round up and kill all the wild horses and cattle that lived near their settlements. Otherwise, there would not have

*Fritz Wikersheim sketched this rough shelter, which is in the vicinity of Arroyo de los Alamitos, near San José. Structures like these provided temporary shelter for ranch hands.*

been enough food for the colonists' herds. This was a big job. By 1800, there were more than 100,000 wild cattle and horses in the coastal areas. Sometimes the ranchers were forced to reduce the size of their own herds to save enough grass for some of the animals to survive into the next year.

Periods of flooding were almost as big a disaster for the farmers as years with little or no rain. The pounding rains sometimes washed away their crops, and even their homes. There was little the townspeople could do but take out their tools and start again.

Healthcare was a major problem for the Californians. The townspeople and ranchers caught many diseases and were often hurt in accidents. Because of untreated health problems, most townspeople and ranchers did not live past the age of 50.

Although the settlers washed their eating utensils and clothing and bathed more often than did most people who lived during this time period, they did not understand that microscopic creatures, such as germs, spread illnesses. It would take many years before scientists discovered how these germs affected people. Many diseases that we can easily stop today spread rapidly back then.

None of the towns or ranches had a doctor. The only medical specialist a sick person was likely to find was a folk doctor. These healers were usually older women who collected plants for medicinal purposes.

## Militia Duty

Not all the Indians who lived near the colonists decided to move to the missions or work for the settlers. Some of the Native Americans fiercely resisted what they believed was an invasion of their homeland. The settlers were also afraid that some other European nation might invade California. When there was danger of an Indian attack or invasion, the local presidio commander could order the settlers to serve in the militia. The men had to report at the

*Some of the Native Americans in California accepted the Spanish settlers, but many felt that their homeland was being invaded and that they must protect it. This detail of a sketch, probably by José Cardero, is in the collection of the Museo Naval in Madrid. Here a Spanish soldier attacks a group of Native Americans. This is the first known illustration of a California soldier in action.*

town square with their horses and weapons. Most of the settlers owned arms similar to those used by the presidio soldiers. The weapons included lances, swords, and muskets. The presidio commanders usually required the militia from the towns and ranches to serve for at least a few weeks each year. The army officers always allowed the settlers to go home during important work periods, such as cattle roundups, harvest time, and planting.

# The Lives of the Women Settlers

The lives of the women who lived in the towns and ranches were no less difficult than those of the men. Women did most of the work that took place at home and often helped the men in the fields and on the range.

## Work in the House

Most of the women colonists worked as homemakers. Their daily schedules at home paralleled those of the men. Many women had to get up before dawn to fix their families' breakfasts. After the meal, they began their housework. During the late morning, the women prepared the main meal of the day. After serving the food at about 12:00 P.M., they spent the next few hours either resting or socializing with family members and friends. Then they went back to work. During the final hours of daylight, they prepared the evening meal.

Many hours were spent preparing food and cooking. The women used stones called manos and metates to grind grain into flour. The larger slabs of stone, called metates, were shaped like big, open-ended bowls. The smaller stones, called manos, were fist-sized rocks that were shaped like bars of soap. The settlers rocked the manos back and forth to grind the grain into powder. Every home had its own stove. Several families usually shared a large oven.

*A woman reenactor, or a specialist in living history, prepares food using some of the same kinds of tools that were used in early California towns.* ▶

*An outdoor oven, or horno, such as this one, located next to a home in the San Pasqual Valley, would have been used by several families in the pueblos.*

The women were in charge of preserving each family's food. The period that followed harvesting was particularly hectic. One way to preserve the harvest bounty was to dry the fruits and vegetables to be eaten during the winter months. It took many days to cut and hang the vegetables and fruits for drying. The women braided together some of the items, such as chilies, into long strings using their stems. Other plants were tied together into clusters. The resulting bunches were suspended from the roof beams and wooden pegs set into the walls.

The families had to work many hours to butcher a large animal, such as a cow. The men and boys stripped away the animal's skin using sharp knives. The women cut the flesh from the bones in long strips. They often barbecued the hearts and tongues right away, but most of the meat was dried for later use. Everyone worked together to dip the thin slices in salt. The ribbons of meat were hung on poles, ropes, and even tree branches to dry. The ranchers and townspeople usually stored the meat in their small homes. They often illegally traded a small portion of the dried product, which was known as *charqui* or *cecina*, to other settlers or Indians.

The women spent many hours cleaning their families' small houses. They used brooms made from reeds and grass to sweep the floors. The women cleaned their cooking equipment using brushes made from dried straw. They also scraped the black grease off their homes' crude oil lamps, and filled the lamps with new grease.

*This cross, found at Mission San Antonio, though not from the mission era, is similar to the religious artifacts used at the time.*

The oldest woman in the household usually took care of the family shrine. It generally consisted of some religious prints or paintings, a crucifix, and some kind of simple altar. The women had to dust every item. They also had to make sure that the candles were kept burning at all times.

The women were responsible for washing the families' clothing, blankets, napkins, sheets, rugs, and tablecloths. They hauled their heavy bundles of laundry to the closest stream or river. Everything was soaked in the water before being beaten with wooden clubs or rocks, and then scrubbed with soap. After rinsing the laundry in the flowing water, the women draped the fabrics on trees or clotheslines to dry.

The women fashioned many useful household products out of the limited supply of materials that was available. Most of the mothers designed and

*Baskets, such as this one from Mission San Antonio, would have been woven by the women to carry food and supplies or to store goods in the home.*

sewed the clothing that their families wore. Many women became famous for their beautiful embroidery. Clothing wore out quickly, so women spent many hours making repairs. The mothers and daughters collected reeds, straw, and grass to construct brushes, brooms, baskets, and trays.

Most married women were responsible for managing their family's money. They were the ones who decided how much of the household's meager income would be used to buy grain and other items. Because they had to keep track of money, these women often mastered basic arithmetic, a skill that most frontiersmen lacked.

## Work Outside the House

In California, women and girls could often be found in the fields working alongside their male family members. Some women whose husbands had died ran their families' farms and ranches. A few women decided not to marry and made their living on their own. Women and girls frequently hunted wild animals for food. They could also be found collecting shellfish and useful wild plants. Many of the older single women worked as part-time tailors, cooks, gardeners, bakers, and weavers.

# Growing Up on the Frontier

Hundreds of youngsters grew up in California's towns and ranches. The size of the typical frontier family ranged from two to more than a dozen people. However, most families had only two or three children. Because of deaths caused by diseases and accidents, there were many families with only one parent. As the towns and ranches grew, the families increasingly included aunts, uncles, and grandparents.

The lives of very young frontier children were very different from those of the adults. Infants spent each day with their mothers. During the first few months of their lives, they were bound in special pieces of fabric called swaddling cloths. These cloths prevented them from crawling or even moving their arms or legs very much. The mothers held their babies while they fed and played with them, but the tiny colonists spent most of their time in cradles that were suspended from the roof using rope. By the time that they were one year old, children were given more freedom. Older relatives usually supervised the youngsters while their mothers worked.

## The Children at Work

When boys and girls turned four, they were given chores to do. The first job that most youngsters had to master was carrying water or firewood for

their mothers. Over time, their parents gave them increasingly difficult jobs that required more responsibility. The older children soon learned how to help out by taking care of their younger brothers and sisters.

As boys and girls grew up, their parents expected them to help out at the same jobs that they did. By the time someone turned fifteen, he or she would have learned how to do most of the basic tasks of daily life. However, children were not considered adults until they were married. Most brides were between fifteen and twenty-one years old. Husbands were usually a few years older than their wives.

## Education at Home

Parents and older family members taught children what they needed to know as adults. Everyone had to learn to ride horses, for example. There was no other way to get from one place to another. There were few trails, and almost no roads. Wolves and bears could be found on the outskirts of all the Spanish settlements. As the boys and girls grew up, the adults taught them how to hunt these dangerous wild animals using lances and ropes.

Not everything that the frontier children learned involved physical education. They grew up surrounded by adults who spoke many different languages. Most of the youngsters learned to speak Spanish and several Indian tongues.

Parents often told their children folktales. These stories taught children lessons about what was right and wrong. The children were supposed to go

◄ *Children worked as apprentices with the adults in the community. In this plate from Denis Diderot's encyclopedia, the child near the center is shown helping to make cast iron by pouring molten iron into molds made out of either sand or fired earthenware.*

to a class on religion that was taught by priests from the nearby missions. However, the missionaries were usually too busy to go to the towns or ranches. As a result, the parents taught their children most of what they knew about their faith. These stories would be passed down through the generations. Some stories are still remembered today by the descendants of these early settlers, and they provide oral historians with information about early California.

## The Town Schools

*This study of King Carlos IV of Spain was done by Francisco José de Goya y Lucientes. It was created in preparation for a royal family portrait.*

During the period that California was settled by Spain, between 1769 and 1821, Europeans began to believe that everyone should attend school. To improve the general quality of life in California, King Carlos IV decided to create schools for everyone who lived in the province. This was a new idea. In most places in the Spanish Empire and the rest of Europe, only the wealthiest people had a chance to attend school.

Many parents who lived in the towns understood the advantages of a formal education, and they sent their children to classes when they could. However, the young people who lived on the ranches were too far away from the towns or other settlements to take advantage of this new opportunity. By 1800, San José and Los Angeles had one-room schools for boys. Each class had about 30 students who were working at several different grade levels.

The California schools did not completely fulfill King Carlos's noble vision. Government officials never managed to start classes for the girls who lived in the towns. After 1810, the government had to spend all of its funds to solve military problems. There was rarely any money to pay the teachers. As a result, the town schools usually had to shut down. After 1821, the government of Mexico made some attempts to revive the school system, but it also ran out of money.

# Entertainment

The Californians had to work hard to survive, but they enjoyed many different kinds of entertainment.

## Entertaining at Home

The townspeople and ranchers spent most of their spare time at home with their families. Some of the entertainments were very simple. Every person above the age of ten smoked cigars and cigarettes. The colonists did not know that tobacco was very bad for their health. Another favorite pastime was drinking hot chocolate. The colonists combined ground chocolate, cinnamon, sugar, and water in tall jars. They used a special wooden tool called a *molinillo* to stir the mixture.

Playing games was another favorite pastime. During the afternoons and the evenings, they often gambled using cards and dice. Not all the pastimes involved wagers. The colonists also loved checkers, backgammon, and chess.

In the evening, the family would take out their musical instruments and sing and dance. Many families owned at least a violin or a guitar. There were hundreds of different popular songs about love and adventure. Sometimes the celebrations would last until after midnight.

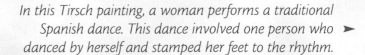

*In this Tirsch painting, a woman performs a traditional Spanish dance. This dance involved one person who danced by herself and stamped her feet to the rhythm.* ➤

auß dem der Mannschen fürkommen Leüthe, wo wir hier froliche allein tantzet, und nach dem Schlag der Zither nach die füß Schlagen müß.

*In this reenactment, settlers gather in the pueblo to discuss the events of the day.*

The colonists held special parties, or fiestas, at the end of harvests, roundups, and other difficult jobs. No one worked on these holidays. The community elders organized special games and other kinds of amusements. In the town square, the colonists watched bullfights, horse races, and fights between wild bulls and grizzly bears. Every fiesta ended with a community dance. These celebrations provided some of the most important, and happy, occasions in the settlers' lives.

## Children's Activities

A number of special kinds of entertainment were reserved for young people. The adults provided their smaller children with toys. The frontier playthings included wooden hobbyhorses, tops, clay marbles, dolls, or *muñecas*, and peashooters. Many different games were popular, such as jacks, hopscotch, and blindman's buff. When they could get them, the children also played with cards and dice. Many of the youngsters' activities involved dancing, riddles, clapping, and songs. Countless evenings were spent listening to the adults sing songs and recite folktales and riddles.

# Frontier Religion

The people who lived on the ranches and in the towns were all Roman Catholics. In contrast with the missions, these settlements did not have their own priests. Instead, the Indians' Franciscan fathers were responsible for meeting their spiritual needs.

It took many years for the towns' settlers to find the time and resources needed to build permanent churches. When they were finally completed, the buildings looked like the other early California temples. They did not have any benches on which people could sit. During different parts of the services, the people stood or kneeled. Just inside the door was a small container of holy water. At one end of the church was a large wooden platform used by the choir. Paintings and statues of saints covered the walls and altars. An image of the saint after which the community was named occupied the position of honor over the main altar.

Not all the religious ceremonies took place at the church. For the devout settlers, the day usually began and ended with the lighting of candles and family prayers. The oldest male would wake up his family by singing a hymn. As the other members of the household woke up, they joined in. Most of the colonists also wore crosses or carried other similar religious Catholic objects. These items reminded them of their religion.

◄ *This drawing of Mission San Luis Rey in the late 1820s, by Auguste Duhaut-Cilly, shows how large the churches were compared to the rest of the buildings. Churches were usually the largest structures in the settlements.*

The Franciscans were kept very busy by taking care of the needs of the mission Indians and presidio inhabitants. They rarely had a chance to visit the towns or their chapels. Because the priests were rarely present, the families organized many ceremonies with very little help from outsiders.

## The Religious Fiestas

Religious holidays often went on for several days. Many of the celebrations involved special ceremonies inside the church, solemn religious

*A modern statue of Saint Joseph stands in the garden at Mission San Diego de Alcalá. The oldest of California's Spanish missions, San Diego de Alcalá was dedicated in 1769 by the Franciscan padre Junípero Serra.*

parades, and many hours of silent prayers. However, the ceremonies were not all serious. Many religious holidays included festive parties.

The townspeople spent weeks preparing for the most important fiestas. The women decorated the church and their families' shrines with beautiful flowers. The men cut tree branches from trees to beautify the outsides of their homes.

The townspeople put on a particularly lavish celebration for San Isidro, the patron saint of the peasants. The priests taught that this saint was the friend of all farmers. The day began with a solemn mass. The townspeople took the statue of San Isidro for a visit to each of the community's homes and fields. At each stop, the settlers offered special prayers, songs, drinks, and food to honor the saint. Late in the afternoon, the colonists returned the saint's statue to its place in the church. The townspeople finished the day with a community dance.

# The Californio Heritage

The missionaries disliked and distrusted the townspeople and ranchers. They did not want them in California. Many townspeople and ranchers grew to dislike the priests, the mission Indians, and the military government of the province. They wanted more freedom, the right to rule themselves, and land. As did the American frontiersmen, they believed that the Indians did not have a right to anything that they were not using. As far as the townspeople and ranchers were concerned, California and its riches belonged to them.

Political changes that took place after 1821 gave the ranchers and townspeople control of California. After 1835, the missions were gone. The Franciscans' fears came true. Nearly all the lands that had once been a part of the missions became ranches. The Indians were transformed into homeless people in their own native country. The United States conquered California in 1846. Since then, many hundreds of thousands of newcomers have moved to the region. Countless items that were a part of Spanish and Mexican California are gone. However, some parts of the Californio heritage have survived.

In a very real way, the towns still exist. Los Angeles is the second largest city in the United States. It also has the second largest concentration of people of Mexican heritage to be found anywhere. San José is one of the

◀ *The heritage of the missions is still evident in California today. Here Los Angeles is outlined in blue, San Jose in orange, and San Francisco in red.*

largest cities in the western United States. Branciforte is now a suburb of the rapidly growing town of Santa Cruz.

The ranches of early California, along with those of other parts of northern Mexico, provided much of the technology and technical terms used by later American ranchers. Many of the laws that govern the cattle industry also have Spanish origins. Spain also provided most of the cowboys' myths. The townspeople's and ranchers' ideals of freedom, self-government, and opportunity are still an important part of how modern Californians think about themselves.

The sad treatment of the Indians, which the missionaries fought to prevent, has almost been forgotten. This is also an important part of the Californio heritage that should be remembered. Even now, little has been done to correct the wrongs that the native peoples have suffered.

The story of California's first towns and ranches provides us with a tale of a people's struggle to survive in the face of many challenges. It forms a unique chapter in the bigger story of our shared human experience that deserves to be remembered and respected.

San Francisco Solano

San Rafael Arcángel

Presidio
de San
Francisco

San José

Santa Clara de Asís

Pueblo de San José

Santa Cruz

Pueblo de Branciforte

San Juan Bautista

Presidio de
San Carlos
de Monterey

San Carlos Borromeo
de Carmelo

Nuestra Señora de la Soledad

San Antonio de Padua

San Miguel Arcángel

San Luis Obispo de Tolosa

La Purísima Concepción

Santa Inés

Santa Bárbara

Presidio de Santa Bárbara

San Buenaventura

San Fernando
Rey de España

Pueblo de
Los Angeles

San Gabriel
Arcángel

San Juan
Capistrano

San Luis Rey
de Francia

Presidio de San Diego

San Diego
de Alcalá

# Glossary

**alcaldes** (ahl-KAHL-des)  Mayors.

**atole** (ah-TOH-lay)  A porridge made from corn and other ingredients, such as meat and vegetables.

**ayuntamientos** (ah-YUN-tah-mee-en-tos)  City councils.

**cecina** (seh-SEEN-ah)  Dried meat.

**charqui** (CHAR-kee)  Another word for dried meat .

**choza** (CHO-zah)  Hut.

**comisionados** (koh-MIH-see-uh-nah-dos)  A commissioner. In California, this term was used for military officers who were put in charge of the towns before 1821.

**cultural anthropologists** (KUL-chuh-ruhl an-thruh-PAH-luh-jists) Scholars of anthropology who focus on the study of the cultures of living peoples.

**devout** (dih-VOWT)  Very religious or dedicated to God.

**estufa** (eh-STOO-fuh)  A stove.

**granaries** (GRAY-nuh-reez)  Buildings where grains are stored.

**land grants** (LAND GRANTS)  Legal documents that give a person ownership of particular places.

**manos** (MA-nohs)  A grinding tool made from stone, used with metates to make corn meal and similar powders.

**manteca** (man-TEK-ah)  Lard, grease, or any other kind of meat drippings.

**metates** (meh-TAH-tays)  A grinding tool made from stone, used with manos to make corn meal and similar powders

**militia** (muh-LIH-shuh)  Part-time soldiers called up during a time of crisis.

**molinillo** (moh-lih-NEE-oh)  A wooden tool used to stir hot chocolate.

**muñecas** (moo-NYAY-kuz)  Dolls.

**Norteños** (nor-TAYN-yohs)  Northerners. This was a term used for the people who lived on the northern frontier of New Spain, including Alta California.

**paisano** (py-ZAH-noh)  People from the same country. This word was usually used to denote frontier farmers.

**pobladores** (poh-bluh-DOR-ays)  People who lived in a town.

**pozole** (puh-ZOH-lay)  A kind of stew made with corn and meat, and sometimes other vegetables.

**presidios** (preh-SEE-dee-ohz)  Military colonies in northern New Spain. In California, all the presidios were protected by fortifications.

**shrine** (SHRYN)  A small place of worship.

**stocks** (STAHKS)  A kind of wooden frame where a person has his or her legs, arms, or hands held in a tight grip.

**swaddling cloths** (SWAHD-ling KLAHTHZ) Pieces of cloth that were wrapped around an infant to prevent it from moving.

**tortillas** (tor-TEE-yuhz) Flat breads made from corn or flour.

**vaqueros** (vah-KAYR-ohs) Cowboys.

# Resources

There are many places where you can learn more about early California and daily life in the pueblos and ranches. The following lists provide information about some of the more important resources.

## Books

Kerr, Daisy. *Keeping Clean a Very Peculiar History*. New York: Franklin Watts, 1995.
Knill, Harry. *Early Los Angeles*. Santa Barbara, CA: Bellephron Books, 1994.

## Museums

Old Town State Historic Park, San Diego. Located at the junctions of Interstates 5 and 8. *This park focuses on a town that grew in the shadow of California's first presidio.*
The Petaluma Adobe. Located at the corner of Highway 116 and Adobe Road. *The Petaluma Adobe was the headquarters of a ranch empire in northern California.*
Pueblo of Los Angeles State Historic Park. Located at 125 Paseo De la Plaza #400. *This park is dedicated to California's second town.*

## Web Sites

Due to the changing nature of Internet links, PowerKids Press has developed an online list of Web sites related to the subject of this book. This site is updated regularly. Please use this link to access the list:
www.powerkidslinks.com/pcm/townran/

# Index

# About the Authors

Dr. Jack Stephen Williams has worked as an archaeologist and historian on various research projects in the United States, Mexico, South America, and Europe. Williams has a particular interest in the Native Americans and early colonization of the Southwest and California. He holds a doctoral degree in anthropology from the University of Arizona, and has written numerous books and articles. Williams lives in San Diego with his wife, Anita G. Cohen-Williams, and his daughter, Louise.

Thomas L. Davis, M.Div, M.A., was first introduced to the California Missions in 1957 by his grandmother. He began to collect books, photos, and other materials about the missions. He has, over the years, assembled a first-class research library about the missions and Spanish North America, and is a respected authority in his field. After ten years of working in the music business, Davis studied for the Catholic priesthood and was ordained for service in Los Angeles, California. Ten years as a Roman Catholic priest saw Father Thom make another life change. He studied at UCLA and California State University, Northridge where he received his M.A. in history. He is a founding member of the California Mission Studies Association and teaches California and Latin American History at College of the Canyons, Santa Clarita, California. Davis lives in Palmdale, California, with his wife, Rebecca, and his son, Graham.